CARTOON

CLIP-ART FOR YOUTH LEADERS

by Ron Wheeler

Baker Book House
Grand Rapids, Michigan 49516

Copyright 1987 by
Baker Book House Company

ISBN: 0-8010-9682-0

Fifth printing, July 1991

Printed in the United States of America

I dedicate this book to Jesus.
May he honor the efforts
of those who created this book
by using it to glorify his name
and to further his kingdom.

Contents

HOW TO USE CLIP ART

This clip-art book contains hundreds of cartoons that will enhance the effectiveness of youth leaders. Use them to illustrate

newsletters	postcards
posters	overhead transparencies
bulletins	fliers
T-shirts	greeting cards
tickets	newspaper ads
brochures	letterheads
programs	handouts
book covers	stickers
mailers	buttons
balloons	book covers

Clearly there are nearly as many places to use clip art as there are cartoon selections in this book. Let your imagination run wild.

So how do you use clip art? Here are a few helpful hints:

1. *Do not clip the art you plan to use directly from this book.* Most youth ministers have access to a copying machine that makes clear enlargement or reduction copies (or a "fast-print" shop can do this). Clip from the copy, not the book. That way you can use the same drawing again on another occasion.

2. When searching for the right clip art, take advantage of the format of this book. If you need something to draw attention to an item in your newsletter, check the chapter titled, "Attention-Gettin' Headers." If you need something to fill a blank space, try "Spirit-Filled Fillers." If you are looking for an idea for a party, you may find it in "Party Promos" or "Food Events." An index has been provided to facilitate your search.

3. When you clip out the cartoon, allow a little white space around it.

4. Be creative in the use of this clip art. Feel free to cut apart or combine clip art from different sections to create the effect you want. For example, if your group has an annual pig roast and you want to promote it as a really big event, you can make a customized T-shirt or poster design. Start with the pig roast logo in Chapter 5, spell out the location of the event from the letters in Chapter 11, and add the date of the event from Chapter 10. You can promote the event by reducing the whole design and dropping it into your newsletter under the heading, "Don't Miss This!" from Chapter 2.

5. Sketch out where you want the clip art and the other elements before gluing them down. That way you will make sure everything fits and looks right.
6. Scotch tape or glue (using rubber cement) your elements onto stiff white board or light blue graph board. The graph board will help you keep your lines straight, yet won't show up when reproduced.
7. Be sure to eliminate any stray marks or pencil lines that may show up when reproduced.

That should cover it. Have fun!

ATTENTION GETTIN' HEADERS

Do you want to draw special attention to a specific item in your newsletter? Have you had difficulty getting people to sign up or pay when they are supposed to? Or do you simply want to make sure your pearls of wisdom don't fall on deaf ears? This chapter will help you make sure your message is read. Also included are various coupons and tickets that can easily be customized.

9

THIS'LL GRAB YA!

HOLD EVERY-THING

SHHHHH! DON'T TELL NOBODY!

WATCH FOR...

WATCH OUT!

WOW!

OH MY LOOK!

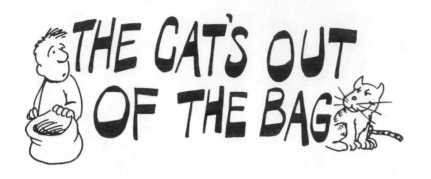

THE CAT'S OUT OF THE BAG

Coming Soon!

COMING ATTRACTIONS

HERE IT IS

TIME'S-A-WASTIN'

HERE'S HOW:

HURRY! HURRY!

Sign Up Early

DON'T MISS THIS

DON'T MISS OUT!

SNIPF

CHECK IT OUT

IT'S A SURPRISE!

ATTENTION!

LET'S GO!

3 CHEERS FOR...

BELIEVE IT OR NOT!

I BELIEVE!

YOUTH STUFF

TIME'S RUNNING OUT

GROUP SCOOP

HANKS A LOT

JUST A REMINDER!

COUPONS

BUY ONE GET ONE FREE!

DISCOUNT!

FREE!
NO CHARGE AT ALL

2 FER 1

ADMIT ONE (SIN)

FREE FUN!

THIS IS YOUR TICKET TO FUN

PARTY PROMOS

Need an idea for a party? How about a "Semi-formal" where everyone comes dressed like a trucker? Instead of name tags, give everyone CB handles. Perhaps you already have a party theme in mind. If it isn't included in this chapter, check another chapter such as, "Food Events," or "Calendar Fixin's" (holiday parties), for ideas. We have also included some generic party heads so your big event can easily be promoted.

JOKES PARTY

HAY RIDE

APRIL FOOLS PARTY

HOMECOMING

M*A*S*H PARTY

BARN DANCE

SNIPE HUNT

MAD HATTER PARTY

TRIVIAL PURSUIT PARTY

TUFF TIMES

WiLD GOOSE CHASE

MARATHON NIGHT

WATER WARS

MONSTER MASH

SCAVENGER HUNT

ICE "FALL"ees

SPORTS HEADS

Ready to play mix and match? These heads can be used in a variety of ways: to promote an event, to announce practice, or to recruit players. All the lettering styles are compatible with each other so you can choose an opening, add the sport, and drop in the ending. For example, you can say "Let's have a Volleyball Picnic," or "Hey, soccer fans," or "Come to a Flag Football Practice," or "It's Crazee Olympics Time," or simply "Softball Practice."

SPORTS SPECTACULAR

HEY,
IT'S
LET'S
THE

LET'S PLAY
LET'S HAVE A
COME TO A

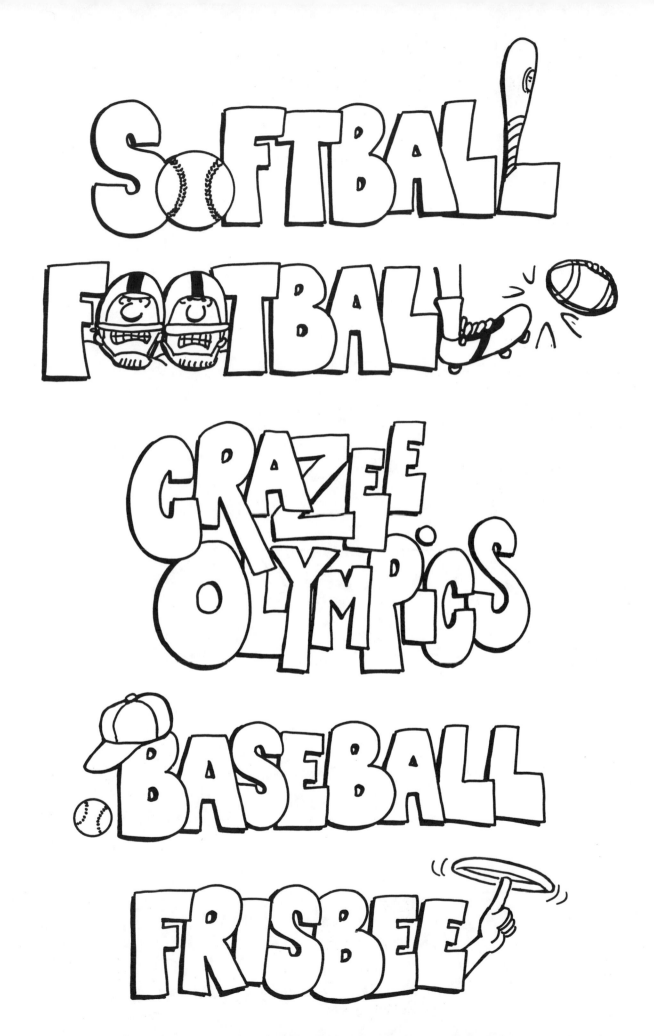

GOLF

TENNIS

WAR BALL

WATER SPORTS

RACQUETBALL

WORLD CUP
PING PONG
SWIMMING
WORLD
CHAMPIONSHIPS
WATER SKI

CHAMPIONSHIP   DAY

PARTY   FANS

GAME   GAMES

PRACTICE   NIGHT

PICNIC   TIME

PLAYERS   FINALS

TOURNAMENT   BUFFS

TEAM

43

SNORT

98

TENNIS (⊙)

FOOD EVENTS

It is a widely known fact that if you want to draw a crowd, serve food. These logos are designed to draw attention to a food event. Included are some generic words such as, "All Church" or "Teen," that will help publicize a specific event.

CHURCH PAN-CAKE FEED

PIZZA BLAST!

BURGER BONANZA

BARBECUE

ICE CREAM SOCIAL

GOOD LUCK POT LUCK

CHOW DOWN

CHOMP CRUNCH CRUNCH

FOOD EVENT!

TEEN YOUTH

CHURCH ALL CHURCH

PIG ROAST

TRIP INFO

Need to drum up some enthusiasm for a future expedition? These cartoons can be enlarged for use on posters and T-shirts or reduced to fit on a calendar or a newsletter. Included are some generic trip heads ("Road Trip," "Hop Aboard") as well as some specific popular trips ("Bike Hike," "Canoe Trip"). Add heads such as "What to Bring" and "Check List." Your trip information will be complete and attractively publicized.

AMUSEMENT PARK TRIP

HIKING

BACK PACKING

SKi TRiP

BIG CITY EXPEDITION

TRIP INFO:

BACK TO NATURE!

BEACH BOUND

YOUTH FUNCTIONS

Rallies, Bible studies, retreats, service projects . . . all the important events that help the spiritual ministry of your group can be advertised with the items in this chapter. Many of the heads have been used by a specific denominational ministry, yet they are general enough to be effective for other youth ministries. Included are some generic words like "Youth" and "Teen," to use with words such as "Club" or "Missions."

YOUTH

TEEN

CLUB

WEEK

MISSIONS

NIGHT

PARENTS DAY

PARENT & TEEN BANQUET

IMPACT!

YOUTH Literature

VACATION BIBLE SCHOOL

HOLY BIBLE

WORK DAY

WORK WEEK

CAR WASH

WALK-A-THON

CANNED FOOD DRIVE

YOUTH MISSION EDUCATION

MUSIC NEWS

A music ministry can be promoted with the use of these cartoons, heads, and logos. The items can be used in such places as an ongoing newsletter column ("Album Review"), bulletin announcements ("Choir Practice"), posters ("Concert!"), or programs ("Singspiration").

SINGALONGATHON

BELL CHOIR

SONG SHINE

CHOIR PRACTICE

JOYFUL SINGERS

CONCERT!

Summer Youth Celebration

YOUTH CHOIR NEWS:

CHRISTMAS CAROLS

SPIRIT FILLED FILLERS

Got a blank spot in your church newsletter that you need to fill? Does your brochure look too boring, busy, and hard to read? Use one of these fillers to make your material sparkle.

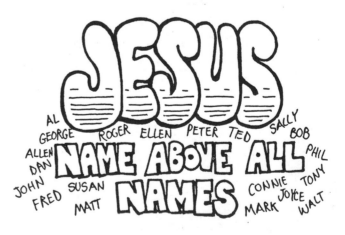

PLUG INTO GOD

THE WALK

ACADEMY OF LOVE

LICENSE TO LOVE

THE SWORD OF THE SPIRIT

REVIVAL

FIGHT THE GOOD FIGHT!

TRUTH

TRUTH

GOD

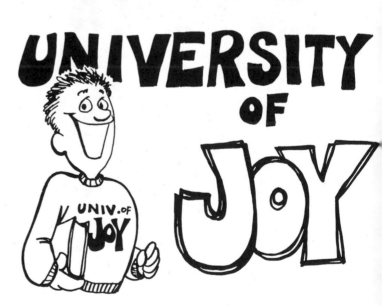

CALENDAR FIXIN'S

This chapter will give a lot of help. There are holiday ("Valentine's Day") and special occasion ("Summer's Here") cartoon logos. There are generic one-month, three-month, and yearly calendars ready for customizing with specific events for any year or month. There are seasonal gag cartoons and several general usage words and numbers. Combine items to construct custom headers, such as: "Friday Night Live," or "Wednesday Morning Prayer Breakfast." These items can also be used to customize cartoon logos from previous chapters, such as "Ski Trip, December 14–20," or "Youth Rally, Friday Night."

FRIDAY NIGHT LIVE

BACK TO School!

CONGRATULATION GRADUATION

HALLOWEEN

THANKSGIVING

SUMMER'S HERE!

MEMORIAL DAY

Birthdays.

BECAUSE IT'S...
"MUTT HAIRS" DAY!

HAPPY MUTT HAIRS DAY!

HERE'S A WILD AND CRAZEE "HAPPEE BIRDEE" TOOO YOOO!

HAVE A BIG "PAW" DAY

MONDAY:

TUESDAY:

WEDNESDAY:

THURSDAY:

FRIDAY:

SATURDAY:

SUNDAY:

BIRTHDAYS:

MONDAY	APRIL
TUESDAY	MAY
WEDNESDAY	JUNE
THURSDAY	JULY
FRIDAY	AUGUST
SATURDAY	SEPTEMBER
SUNDAY	OCTOBER
JANUARY	NOVEMBER
FEBRUARY	DECEMBER
MARCH	MONTH
DAY YEAR	1987 8 9 0 1

BREAKFAST

LUNCH

DINNER

SNACK

BRUNCH

SUPPER

FELLOWSHIP

BIBLE STUDY

MEETING

LIVE

PRAYER

PARTY

PRAISE

NIGHT

EVENING

AFTERNOON

NOON

MORNING

WINTER

SPRING

SUMMER

FALL

JANUARY JUNE

FEBRUARY JULY

SEPTEMBER MAY

OCTOBER APRIL

NOVEMBER

DECEMBER

MARCH AUGUST

SUN	MON	TUES	WED	THURS	FRI	SAT

1 2 3 4 5 6 7 8

9 10 11 12 13 14 15 16

17 18 19 20 21 22 23 24

25 26 27 28 29 30 31 -

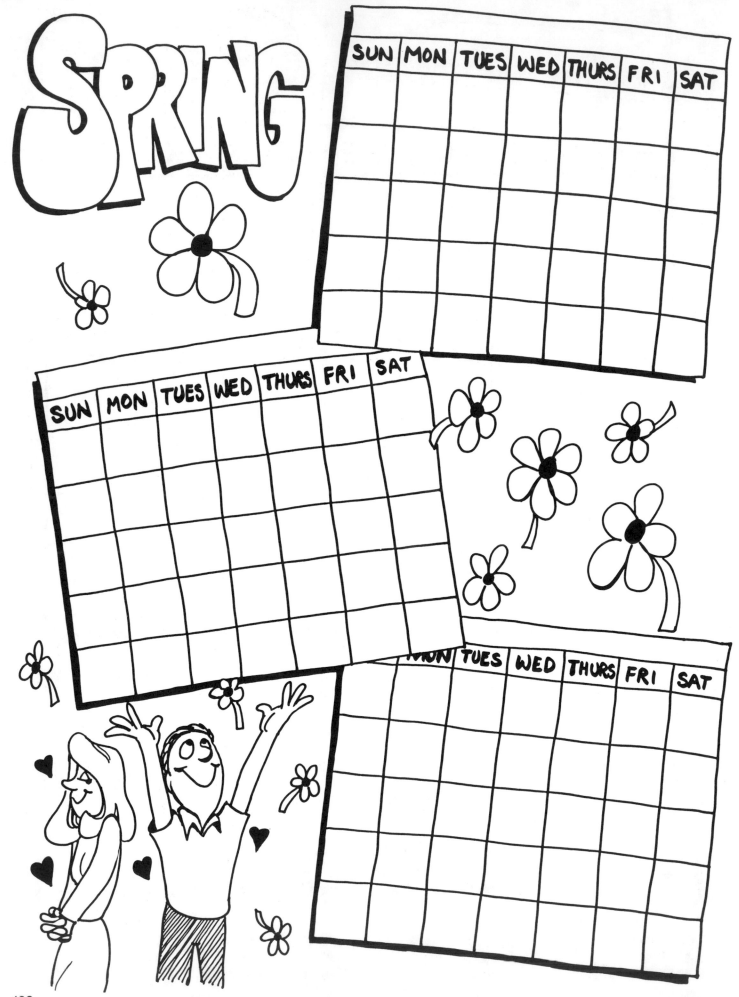

SPRING

SUN	MON	TUES	WED	THURS	FRI	SAT

SUN	MON	TUES	WED	THURS	FRI	SAT

SUN	MON	TUES	WED	THURS	FRI	SAT

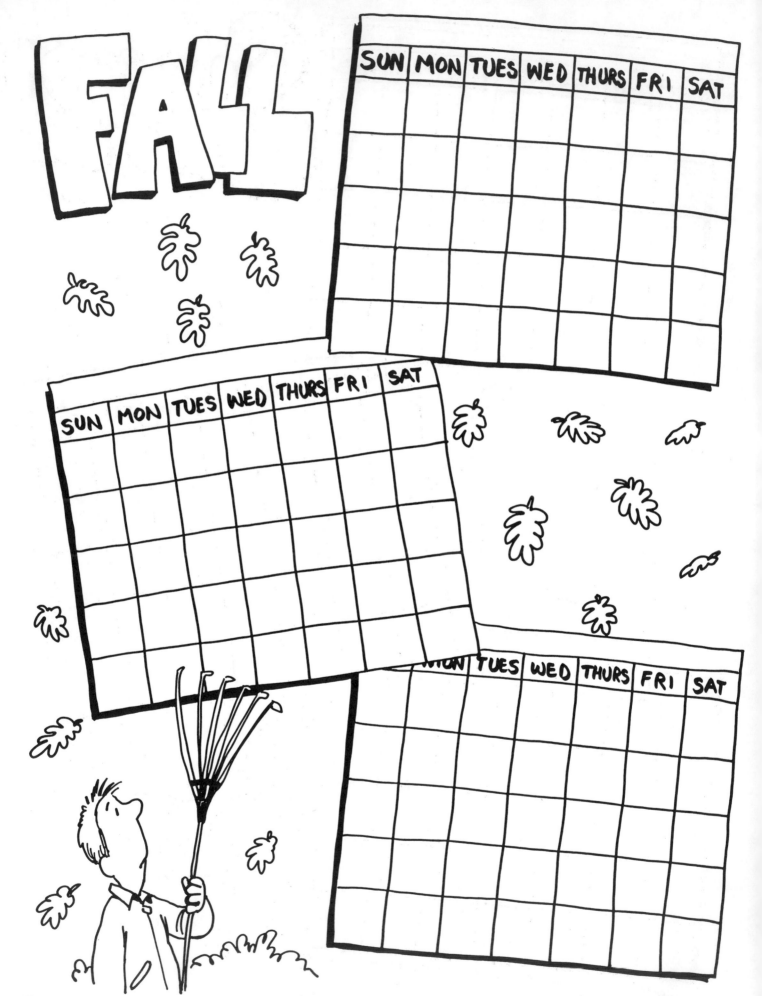

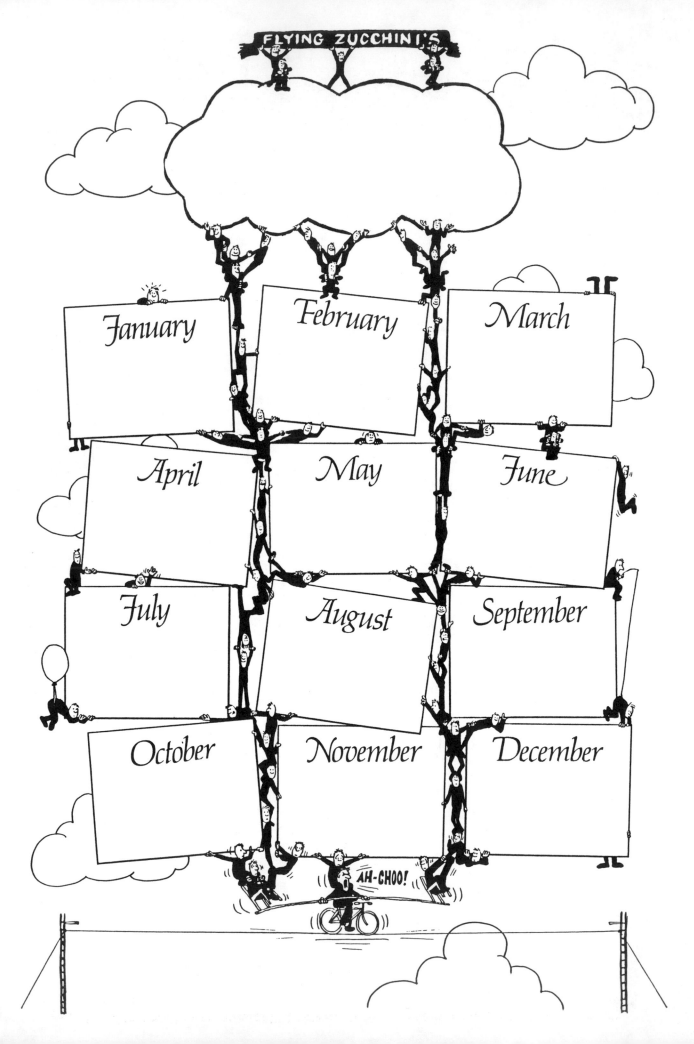

112

115

116

BORDERS, SYMBOLS, & LETTERS

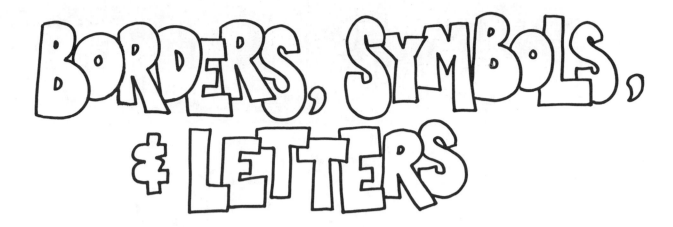

Now you can let your creativity really run wild. This chapter contains a variety of decorative symbols which can be reproduced several times over, and placed together to form borders, boxes, squares, and rectangles. There are also several easy-to-use cartoon-style balloons, banners, and boxes ready to promote your message. If you want to give that message a quality look, use the cartoon lettering alphabets and numbers to make your message. Newsletter, stationery, and postcard mastheads are also included.

This is a good chapter to use in conjunction with other parts of this book. For example, you may want to print some posters with the "Walk Through the Bible" drawing from the "Spirit-Filled Fillers" chapter. Using the symbols and letters from this chapter you could outline the cartoon and customize it with your church name. This technique could also be used to enhance and customize T-shirt designs, posters, and even handouts. A typical example could be a T-shirt advertising "Colonial Church River Ride, August, 1988."

NEWSLETTER

YOUTH NEWS

TEEN-REPORT

A SPECIAL MESSAGE  FROM YOUR LEADER

 A SHORT NOTE!

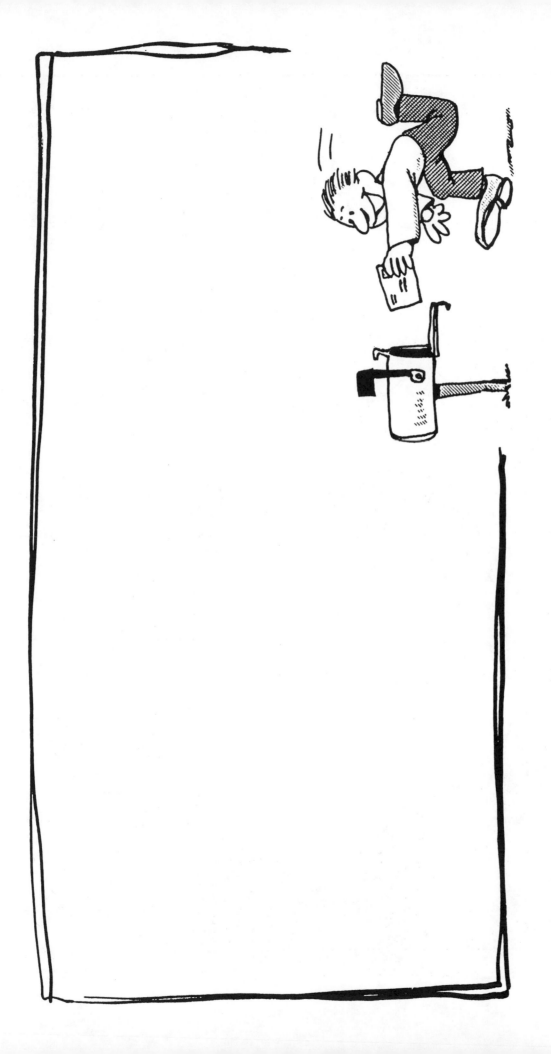

HELEN.

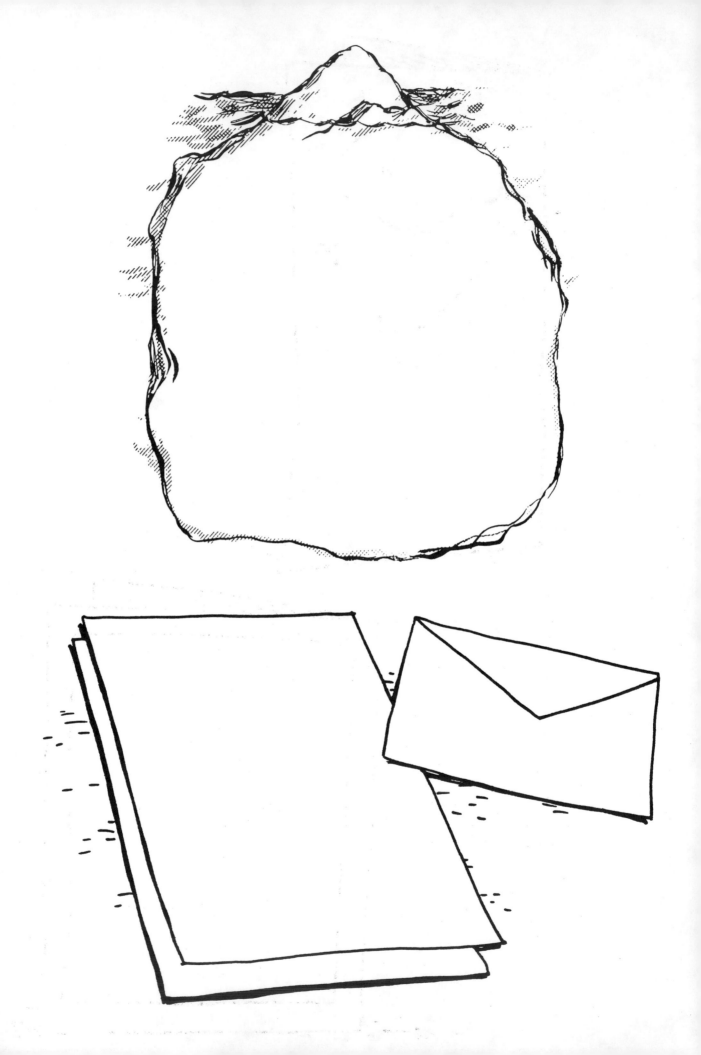

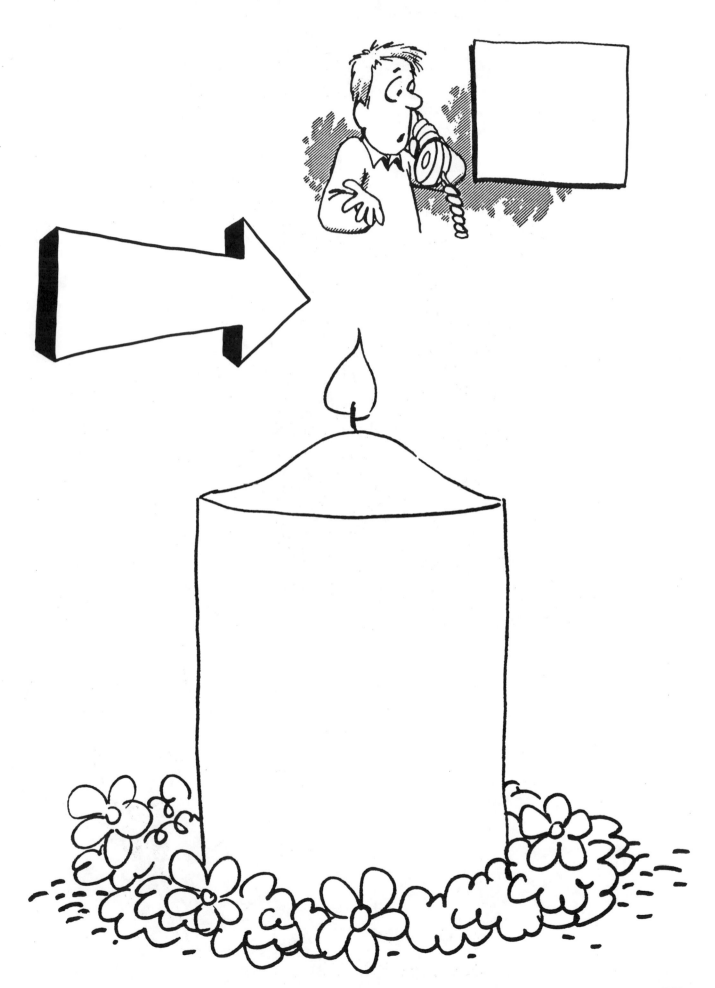

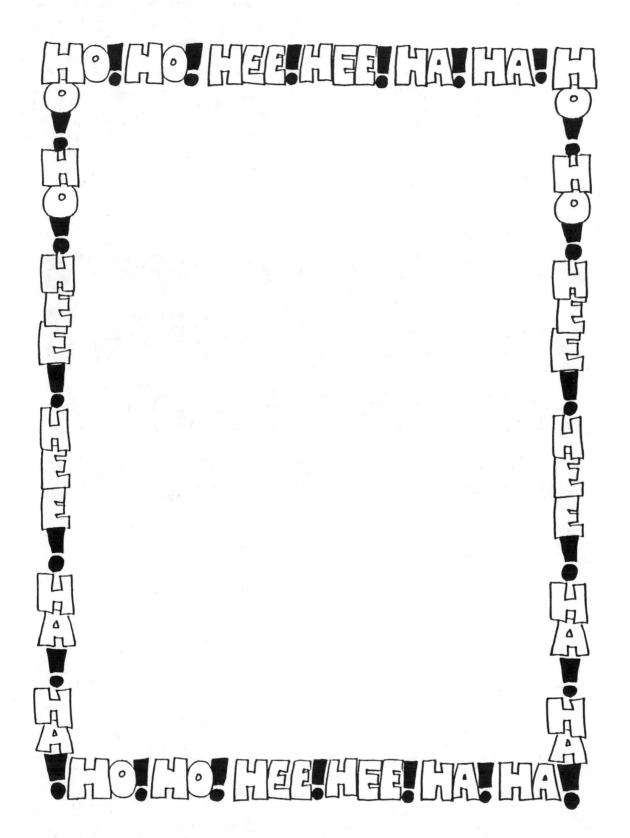

ABCDEFGHIJKL
MNOPQRSTUVW
XYZ?!"$#12345
67890

abcdefghijklmnopqrs
tuvwxyzABCDEFGH
IJKLMNOPQRSTUV
WXYZ?!",$#123456
7890

ABCDEFGHIJKL
MNOPQRSTUVW
XYZ?!"$#1234
567890

ALL PURPOSE SPOT CARTOONS

This chapter has a variety of fun cartoons that do not readily fit into any of the other sections. Use them as space fillers, and to illustrate announcements in your newsletter.

"We'll Knock Your Socks Off!"

OFFICIAL EXECUTIVE
SENIOR VICE PRESIDENT
IN CHARGE OF
LOADING STAPLERS.

153

154

HAVE YOU SEEN IT?

You Were Destined to Break Records, Not Save Them!

WELL ROUNDED TEEN
BELIEVER

GETTING A HANDLE ON SCHOOL

HOW DO YOU SPELL...

EVANGELISM

INDEX